To Simon and Lee for their friendship and
long-suffering stewardship of the Manc Rs.
C.G.

For all the kids in the world, this is just
a peek at the amazing things you can do.
L.A.

First published in Great Britain 2023 by Red Shed, part of Farshore

An imprint of HarperCollins*Publishers*
1 London Bridge Street, London SE1 9GF
www.farshore.co.uk

HarperCollins*Publishers*
Macken House, 39/40 Mayor Street Upper,
Dublin 1, D01 C9W8

Copyright © HarperCollins*Publishers* Limited 2023

ISBN 978 0 00 860610 7

Printed and bound in the UK using 100% Renewable Electricity at CPI Group (UK) Ltd.

001

A CIP catalogue record for this title is available from the British Library.

MIX
Paper | Supporting
responsible forestry
FSC™ C007454

INCREDIBLE
FOOTBALL

Written by Clive Gifford
Illustrations by Lu Andrade

RED■
SHED

"In football, everything is possible, from the moment you work and you believe in your qualities."

– Kylian Mbappé

Contents

Introduction

Football is the world most popular team sport and with good reason. It's fast, sometimes furious, and often full of flair, skill and drama. The top players are global superstars and big matches are watched by hundreds of millions.

This book is packed with amazing stories and incredible facts about extraordinary players, mega matches, fantastic fans, much-loved mascots, and unforgettable moments. From the referee who sent himself off, to the refugee-turned-football superstar; from the defender who had a run-in with a moose, to the striker sold for his weight in shrimp, this book is stuffed full of footballing fun.

In addition to discovering football's most exciting

stories, you'll also find a glossary that explains key footballing terms, a simple guide to the rules of the game, plus player profiles and a quiz to test your knowledge.

So, wherever you are on your football journey, we hope you have fun!

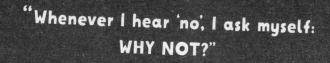

Seeing Red, Red, Red . . .

Referee Damian Rubino holds a red card record.
In an Argentinean league game between Victoriano
Arenas and Club Atlético Claypole, he sent off ALL
22 PLAYERS after a mass bundle broke out.

If that wasn't enough, the ref *also* showed his red card
to substitutes, coaches and assistants, making
a grand total of 36 sendings-off! Match abandoned!

DID YOU KNOW?

Referee Osman Tosum forgot to bring his
red card with him when refereeing an English
non-league match in 2008. So he improvised
and used an orange till receipt from a DIY
store as a red card when he had to send
a player off!

Quick, Quick, Kylian!

Pace is important for a striker and few are faster than the great France and Paris Saint-Germain (PSG) star Kylian Mbappé. During a 2019 match against AS Monaco, Kylian reached an ultra rapid 38kmph. That's actually 0.4kmph faster than Usain Bolt's average speed when he broke the world 100m sprint record in 2009!

Major Impact

Let's travel back in time to the 1900s. Major the dog was the much-loved pet of Newton Heath LYR (Lancashire & Yorkshire Railway) football club captain Harry Stafford. The club was in desperate financial trouble and the large Saint Bernard was sometimes sent trotting around the stadium with a collection box fitted to his collar. The club needed all the donations they could get – and who better to encourage fans to reach into their pockets than a football-loving dog!

In 1901, the cash-strapped club held a fund-raising fair. It didn't raise much and, worse still, Major went missing. Disaster! Harry eventually found him with local businessman John Henry Davies, who offered to buy the friendly dog for his daughter. Desperate to keep the football club afloat, Harry agreed to part with his beloved pooch and the businessman became chairman of the club, investing £500 (worth around £50,000 at the time) to keep it going. The following year Newton Heath was renamed . . . **Manchester United.** Yes, THE Manchester United. That makes Major the only dog to have saved a world-famous football club!

From Reject to Select

You would be amazed at some of the top, top players who have been rejected or released by football clubs in the past.

Manchester City turned down both Marcus Rashford and Ryan Giggs for either being too small or not good enough. They went on to become legends across the city at Manchester United.

The incomparable Lionel Messi was rejected by Argentinean club River Plate, whilst Portuguese club Porto released João Félix as a teenager for being too lightweight. A few years later, João was one of the hottest properties in world soccer and sold for £113 million to Atlético Madrid!

Legendary Brazilian striker Ronaldo was heartbroken

when he was turned down by Flamengo – his favourite club and home of his idol, Zico. Months later, he joined Cruzeiro and scored 44 goals in just 47 games, kickstarting a career which included winning the World Cup twice and being voted FIFA World Player of the Year three times. Tough luck, Flamengo!

Spurs and England captain, and goal machine, Harry Kane – yes, THE, Harry Kane – was also let go as a child player. Can you guess by which club?

Arsenal - Spurs' bitter rivals!

Harry was delighted to join the Gunners Academy, run by Arsenal legend Liam Brady. But he was released just a year later. His coach said that he "wasn't very athletic". The rejection hurt Harry but he wasn't going to give up just like that.

"Arsenal's decision to release me
left me with a strong desire
to prove the club wrong."

– Harry Kane

Harry had to fight to get a place at Spurs. The club rejected him on a trial and it was only when he starred in a youth game against them that Spurs finally gave him a chance.

As he grew older, Harry had to not only work hard but be incredibly patient. The seasons ticked by as Spurs loaned him out to four other clubs: Leyton Orient, Millwall, Norwich and Leicester City, before he got a proper chance in the Spurs first team.

In April 2014, he finally made his Premier League debut and seized the chance with both hands. He scored in his first match and, by the start of 2023, had netted 273 goals for the club. These include scoring 14 times (so far) against Arsenal – the club who had rejected him!

Panenka's Big Gamble

There are very few moves in football named after
an individual player. Even fewer started out as the
last kick of a game in a major competition . . .

In 1976, Czechoslovakia* had defied the odds to
reach the final of the UEFA European Championships.
There, they faced a mighty West German side,
defending European champions and winners of the
World Cup two years earlier.

Playing in the Czech midfield was Antonín Panenka.
He was known in his country as a stalwart with the
Bohemians Prague club, but was unknown to many
football fans outside Czechoslovakia. Antonín
poured his heart and soul into the game that day,
as did the whole Czech side, who found themselves

*Czechoslovakia is now two countries, the Czech Republic and Slovakia.
East and West Germany were reunited as a single country in 1991.

in dreamland when they went two goals up after 25 minutes.

Three minutes later, Dieter Müller pulled one back for West Germany. Things got tense. The Czechs held out till deep into the second half. The game was exhausting and concentration had to remain high: one mistake, one loss of focus, and Germany could equalise. In the Czech goal, Ivo Viktor pulled off a string of outstanding saves to keep the Germans out. But he was powerless to stop Bernd Hölzenbein scoring with a close-range header from an 89th minute corner. Now the score was 2–2.

Extra time didn't yield a winner so the game went to a penalty shootout – the first one in history to settle a major competition. With the score at 4–3 to the Czechs, Antonín was designated to take the fifth, potentially decisive, penalty. Some of his teammates knew what he planned to do and begged him not to!

As Antonín placed the ball down on the penalty spot, his team-mates stared at him nervously. Facing him, 11m away, was arguably the world's best goalkeeper, Sepp Maier. He appeared huge and commanding. He seemed to fill up the goal. The pressure was intense.

Most players in the 1970s blasted their penalty shots as hard as they could, low or high, to the right or left corners of the goal. Antonín had a different idea. Cool as you like, he ran up and lightly chipped the ball so it floated down the middle. Sepp Maier, expecting a blasted penalty, dived sharply to his left . . . and the ball gently bounced into the middle of the net!

"It was the work of either a genius or a madman."
– Pelé on Antonín Panenka's penalty

Audacious Antonín had helped Czechoslovakia win their first ever major championship. The chipped or floated penalty down the middle is now known as a 'Panenka' and has been attempted successfully by many of the game's greats, including Andrea Pirlo, Karim Benzema and Lionel Messi. Zinedine Zidane even scored a Panenka in the 2006 World Cup final.

"I suspect that he [Maier] doesn't like the sound of my name too much," said Antonín many years later. "I never wished to make him look ridiculous. On the contrary, I chose the penalty because I saw and realised it was the easiest and simplest recipe for scoring a goal."

THE CRUYFF TURN

The Cruyff turn is where the ball is dragged behind the player to change direction and fool a defender. People raved about Dutch maestro Johan Cruyff performing this move at the 1974 World Cup versus Sweden. It was the first time many people had seen anything like it. However, five days earlier, Australian forward Adrian Alston had performed the exact same trick at the same tournament, versus East Germany!

You can go even further back to 1960 to see an early example of the Cruyff turn and how lethal it could be. A young Pelé performed the move then hit a bullet shot that sailed into the goal of Italian champions Juventus.

North Versus South

The first official women's football match featured just one club! The British Ladies Football Club was formed by Nettie J. Honeyball* in 1894. She placed adverts in newspapers for like-minded women to join the club.

"There is no reason why football should not be played by women, and played well, too."

– Nettie J. Honeyball

Attracting around 30 players, the club split into two teams, North and South, to play their first match the following year. The game drew a crowd of 10,000 spectators. North won 7–1. Despite some rude reviews in the newspapers – not everyone approved of women playing football – the club went on tour, playing around 100 matches before disbanding.

* Not her real name. In fact, we don't know who she was.
After the British Ladies Football Club disbanded, 'Nettie' disappeared!

Brolly Good

Early football was played in some weird kit, from hats and long trousers to suit jackets and riding boots. By 1900, kits with shirts, very long shorts and long socks were in – but that didn't stop Aston Villa winger Charlie Athersmith from accessorising his outfit.

In 1901, during a bitterly cold game versus Sheffield United, freezing rain fell. Some of the Aston Villa players complained of frostbite afterwards. Not Charlie though . . . He borrowed a brolly from one of the spectators and continued playing with one hand holding up the umbrella to shield him from the rain!

In goal for Charlie's opponents that day was another eccentric English player, the legendary William Foulke. The Sheffield United stopper was a man

mountain and a scary keeper to play against.
In fact, he was known to pick opponents up and
either bundle them into his goal net or dangle them
just above the muddy ground if they annoyed him!
Ouch!

Conman Carlos

It was eight minutes into a Brazilian league match in the mid-1980s and the home team, Bangu, were already two goals down. With fans getting restless, the club's owner sent a message from the stands to the manager, Moisés Matias de Andrade. It said: "Bring on Kaiser!"

Carlos Kaiser (real name Carlos Henrique Raposo) was in the final week of his contract with Bangu, but had never played a game, always complaining of an injury. Had his big moment finally come? Would the fans finally get to see him in action for the first time?

Carlos began warming up by jogging along the touchline. But just as it looked like he was about to make his way onto the pitch for his long-awaited debut . . . he picked a fight with some fans and the referee showed him the red card! Carlos was sent off before he'd even stepped on the pitch. Disaster!

Or was it? It turned out Carlos was a conman who had convinced more than a dozen football clubs, mainly in South America, and including big Brazilian sides like Flamengo and Botafogo, to sign and pay him as a professional footballer. He would always feign injury or some other problem before he actually had to play. The reason was simple – he wasn't very good at football!

But Carlos looked the part and could talk a good game. He made friends with footballers, club officials and journalists wherever he went. He told tall stories to get people on his side. So, when Bangu's club owner quizzed him about the fight, Carlos said that he had heard supporters calling the owner nasty names and had to defend the owner's honour! It was a lie, but instead of being reprimanded, or even fired, Carlos got a new contract and a pay rise. Triumph!

"I wanted to be among the other players, I just didn't want to play!"

– Carlos Kaiser

In the 1980s, there was no World Wide Web, social media or smartphones, so news about this footballing imposter didn't spread fast. As a result, cunning Carlos managed to keep the con going at different clubs for – wait for it – 24 years! At the end of his career, he even returned to some of his former clubs. They knew what he was up to, but liked having him around. When he finally 'retired' in 2003, he had managed to avoid playing a single competitive game. Outrageous!

Sister Act

Kristie Mewis had been out of the US national team for more than six years when she was called up again in 2020. Her first match back was a friendly against the Netherlands. Kristie came on in the second half, scoring in the 70th minute to help secure a 2–0 victory. It had been whopping 2,722 days since her last international goal, in 2013 against South Korea!

She didn't have to wait long for her next goal though. It was only 52 days until Kristie scored again, this time against Colombia. But it was her sister, Sam, who stole the limelight in this match, scoring a hat-trick. The US won 4–0, with all four goals being scored by the Mewis sisters!

Black Pioneers

Name: Jack Leslie

Born: London, UK, 1901

Country: England

Clubs: Barking Town, Plymouth Argyle

Position: Inside left (an attacker that flanks the central striker)

Famous for: Being a versatile and free-scoring attacker and a fan favourite at Plymouth Argyle

Although the English league was home to one of the first Black professional footballers – goalkeeper Arthur Wharton in the 1890s – no Black player pulled on an England shirt until the 1970s.

Gifted winger Laurie Cunningham was the first to play for England's Under-21 team in 1977, with defender Viv Anderson the first to debut for the full England team the following year against Czechoslovakia.

Other countries in Europe were well ahead of England. Raoul Diagne was France's first Black player in 1931, whilst Espírito Santo made his debut for Portugal in 1937. Santo was a lethal finisher who won seven league titles with Benfica – as well as being the Portuguese high-jump record-holder for 20 years!

Scotland's first Black footballer was Andrew Watson. He captained the national team to their biggest ever win over England (a 6–1 thrashing) all the way back in 1881. A few days later, he played in Scotland's 5–1 defeat of Wales, followed by another 5–1 victory over England the year after. Andrew could have gone on to play many more times for Scotland, but he moved south of the border to London, and the team selectors at the time only picked players living in Scotland.

In 1925, England nearly had its first Black international player when Jack Leslie was called up for the England team for a match in Belfast. Jack played for Plymouth Argyle, scoring 133 goals for the side in the league alone, and was the first Black player to captain an English professional club.

> **"It was quite a thing for a little club like Plymouth to have a man called up for England. Everybody in the club knew about it. The town was full of it."**
>
> – Jack Leslie

But Jack never travelled with the team and he never got to play. Was he injured? No, it was something more sinister . . . It's thought that some members of the England selection committee had picked Jack from written reports and changed their mind when they realised he wasn't white. Truly scandalous.

> **"Everyone stopped talking about it . . . Didn't look me in the eye. I didn't ask outright. I could see by their faces it was awkward. But I did hear the FA had come to have another look at me. Not at [my] football but at [my] face."**

Jack was never selected for England again. It was only in 2022 that the English FA admitted the mistake and awarded him an honorary England cap. Plymouth fans hadn't forgotten him. His statue adorns Plymouth's ground, Home Park.

For many years, the record of the first Black footballer to actually play for an England team was also forgotten about. Benjamin Odeje was born in Nigeria but moved with his parents to south-east London as a child. There, he played for a variety of teams and, in 1971, aged 15, he was called up to play for England Schoolboys. He was understandably nervous walking out onto the Wembley pitch to play

Northern Ireland on 6th March. After all, there were some 70,000 fans in the stadium. Benjamin said: "I remember being in the Wembley changing room and the phone was handed to me. It was my teacher, Mr Wind. He said, 'Good luck, son.' That made my year."

Benjamin needn't have worried. He had a great game. England won and he was made player of the match. He played five times for England Schoolboys but didn't make it in professional football as an adult. He did, though, become a coach at Queens Park Rangers, a PE teacher and ran his own soccer school. It annoyed him that when his own children mentioned at school how their dad had played for England, no one believed them. But, in 2022, the FA finally recognised his achievements. They invited Benjamin to Wembley to watch a match and updated their record books . . . About time!

Huffing and Puffing

The stadium of Slovakian football club TJ Tatran Čierny Balog has an unusual additional feature – a railway line running through it! The Čierny Hron Railway runs between the pitch and one of the stands. Spectators' views of the game are sometimes obscured by puffs of smoke belching from the steam trains that trundle along the track!

Croc Shock

Turkish side Bursapor are, we think, the only football club in the world that plays in a stadium shaped like a crocodile! The Bursa Metropolitan Stadium has a crocodile's head, its open mouth forming space for a banqueting hall and conference rooms. The ground, which holds over 43,700 spectators, matches the team's nickname of the Green Crocodiles. On match days, the eyes light up for added effect!

DID YOU KNOW?

In 1999, Italian club Fiorentina offered fans some unusual merchandise: three types of tin can containing air from its stadium. These were labelled Air of the Terraces, Essence of Victory and Dressing Room Atmosphere. Poo-eee!

Haaland's Haul

Teenager striker Erling Braut Haaland was not well-known outside of his native Norway . . . until he did something very special at the 2019 FIFA Under-20 World Cup in Poland. Having lost to Uruguay and New Zealand, Norway were set to play their third group stage match against Honduras. Honduras had lost their previous match (2–0 to Uruguay) but against Norway they didn't know what had hit them . . .

Erling scored in the – deep breath – 7th, 20th, 36th (a penalty), 43rd, 50th, 67th, 77th, 88th and 90th minutes. Norway won 12–0 and their tall striker had scored nine of them!

Despite not scoring in any other games during

the tournament, Erling won the Golden Boot as the tournament's top-scorer. Overall, he bagged five more goals than any other player.

Now playing for the full Norwegian team, Erling is still scoring at a rapid rate: 21 goals so far in just 23 games. And at club level, he has bagged over 200 goals in a mere 240 games for sides in Norway, Austria, Germany and, currently, England.

DID YOU KNOW?

Erling was born in Leeds and could have qualified to play upfront for England. Imagine a strike force of Haaland, Harry Kane and Marcus Rashford . . . crazy!

Marvellous Marta

When Cristiano Ronaldo scored in Qatar in 2022, he became the first to score in five successive FIFA World Cups – and the media went wild. They were only half right. Ronaldo, CR7, was the first *man* to do so. Three years earlier, Marta Vieira da Silva had achieved the same feat when she scored against Australia in the 2019 Women's World Cup.

It was just one of 115 goals the Brazilian legend has scored for her country during her long career. She's actually scored a quarter of ALL Brazil's Women's World Cup goals and is the only player to have won five FIFA World Player of the Year awards in a row. Extraordinary!

Pitching Up

There's precious little spare land in Koh Panyee, a small fishing village in Thailand, so the locals built a floating half-sized pitch on which to play football. It's surrounded on all sides by sea, so when the ball goes out of play, players often have to swim to retrieve it!

Koh Panyee's pitch is not the only strange ground in Thailand. In busy Bangkok, where space is also limited, the Unusual Football Field is a project that has created several non-rectangular pitches using empty space. One pitch goes round corners whilst another has one sideline much longer than the other. They may be unusual, but they're still great fun for people to play casual games on!

Pelé - O Rei

Name: Edson Arantes do Nascimento

Born: Três Corações, Brazil, 1940

Nickname: Pelé

Country: Brazil

Clubs: Santos, New York Cosmos

Position: Striker, occasional attacking midfielder

Famous for: Wowing the world with his charm, personality, and graceful, skilful and imaginative attacking play

People go mad for Messi and Mbappé and nuts about Neymar, but the greatest footballer of all reigned long before them. He was called Edson Arantes do Nascimento, but is better known to the world as Pelé or 'O Rei', meaning 'the King' in Portuguese.

Born to a poor family in Bauru, Brazil, Pelé couldn't afford a football to play with. Instead, he used a rotten grapefruit or stuffed a sock full of newspaper and tied it up with string. Between the ages of six and 11, he worked on the street, selling tea and roasted peanuts, or shining shoes. Any spare time was spent playing football matches and practising his silky skills.

Fortunately, Pelé's footballing prowess was spotted early by a coach called Waldemar de Brito. Waldemar had played for Brazil 18 times, so he knew a thing or two about the game. He was incredibly excited at the gifted youngster. He believed Pelé would become, in his words, "the greatest player in the world".

Waldemar took Pelé to Santos FC in 1956. Pelé was just 15 but scored on his debut, and then spent an incredible 19 seasons at the club. When he finally retired in 1974, Santos retired the number 10 shirt in his honour. But what happened in the 19 years between Pelé's first and last game for Santos? Well, where do we start?

Imagine being just 17 and stepping out into a World Cup final. That's what the teenaged Pelé did in 1958, after scoring a hat-trick in the semi-final against France, the youngest player ever to do so. He scored a further two goals in the final, becoming the only teenager to perform such a feat. As Brazil's captain Hilderaldo Bellini lifted the World Cup trophy, Pelé became the youngest ever World Cup winner. He still is!

Wealthy European teams formed a long queue to sign the teenage sensation, but he was so good, the Brazilian government declared him an official 'national treasure'. This meant he couldn't be transferred out of Brazil!

"Success is no accident. It is hard work, perseverance, learning, studying, sacrifice and, most of all, love of what you are doing or learning to do."

– Pelé

As part of the all-conquering Santos and Brazil teams, Pelé became the most famous sportsperson on the planet. Santos toured the world and opponents marvelled at his skill, bravery, close control and vision. He would often try passes, moves and goal attempts that others thought were impossible. He would let the ball run past him and his opponent, only to regain control in an instant. He made the overhead bicycle kick popular. In many games, his opponents found him simply unplayable!

> **"I told myself before the game: 'He's made of skin and bones just like everyone else.' But I was wrong."**
> – Tarcisio Burgnich, Italian defender who marked Pelé in the 1970 World Cup final

On November 19th each year, Brazil celebrates Pelé Day. It's the date when, in 1969, Pelé scored his 1000th career goal at the enormous Maracanã Stadium in Rio de Janeiro. The crowd swarmed onto the pitch and the game was halted for 20 minutes as fans carried Pelé around the stadium!

But that's not all. O Rei set many footballing records that remain unbroken. These include:

- An incredible 643 goals in 660 competitive games for Santos.

- A brilliant 77 goals in 92 games for Brazil.

- The only player to score 25 goals for his country whilst still a teenager.

- The most goals in a calendar year (1959): an unbelievable 127!

- A world record number of hat-tricks: 92. He also scored four goals in a game (a 'super hat-trick') an extraordinary 30 times!

- A HUGE total of 1,283 goals in his career, including friendlies and tour matches.

DID YOU KNOW?

In 1975, Pelé came out of retirement to play for New York Cosmos in the North American Soccer League (NASL). When he retired for the second time in 1977, fittingly, his last game was New York Cosmos versus Santos. Pelé played a half for each team!

"I sometimes feel as though
football was invented
for this magical player."

– Sir Bobby Charlton,
former England player

Number One Fan

It was a chilly Monday night in December 2012 – and a 500km journey from his home town – but *nothing* was going to stop Arrigo Brovedani from seeing his side Udinese play rivals Sampdoria in Italy's top league, Serie A.

There was a crowd of 15,000 at the Stadio Luigi Ferraris, home of Sampdoria, that night. But as Arrigo arrived, he realised that he was the ONLY Udinese fan at the game. Gulp! He took his place in the away section of the stadium and draped his small club flag over the railings. "When I saw the Udinese players were warming up," Arrigo recalled, "I shouted out to them saying, 'Guys, I'm all alone here. Alone! You can hear me now but you won't be able to hear me once the game starts!'"

Arrigo was right. The game kicked off and the stadium erupted with competitive boos and chants – until the Sampdoria fans realised that Arrigo was all on his lonesome. The jeers turned into cheers and a giant round of applause broke out for the lone away fan.

After that, Arrigo's night got even better. Udinese scored twice to secure an excellent away win. The team came and saluted him at the end of the match. And Sampdoria weren't going to be left out either. Arrigo later said, "They were actually really nice – they offered me food and coffee and the club manager gave me a shirt, which was great."

For a couple of weeks, Arrigo was all over the sports news pages. "I don't think it's that big a story," he said. "There are so many keen fans that really never miss a game, so I'm sure I'm not the first one!"

An E For Geography

Six French football fans felt pretty foolish in 2021 after failing their European geography 'exam'. The fans travelled to Bucharest in Romania in time for their team's EURO 2020 match, only to discover that France were playing Hungary in *Budapest*, not Bucharest, an 820km drive away! "We really need to learn more about Europe," one of the fans said when interviewed. No kidding!

DID YOU KNOW?

Since 2003, fans of German club FC Union Berlin turn up to the team's stadium every Christmas Eve to sing Christmas carols. More than 20,000 people attend and sing their hearts out each year.

High-Rise Fans

Some fans will do anything to see the big game . . .

In 2014, around 30 Bayern Munich fans were in Moscow for a Champions League match against CSKA Moscow. The stadium, called the Arena Khimki, was closed to the public and wasn't admitting spectators. So, the Bayern fans rented the 18th floor of an office building that overlooked the ground in order to watch the match.

The game ended in a 1–0 win for Bayern, and after hearing about the story on social media, the club paid the office rent for their intrepid fans. Win-win!

The Hinderwell Hotshot

Name: Beth Mead

Born: Whitby, UK; 1995

Country: England

Clubs: Arsenal, Sunderland

Position: Forward

Famous for: Being a skilful, creative attacker and prolific goalscorer

When Beth Mead's mum was searching for something for her energetic six-year-old daughter to do, she decided to drop her off with the boy's football team in their village of Hinderwell in Yorkshire.

The coach was worried though. What if the boys played rough? What if they were too good for her?

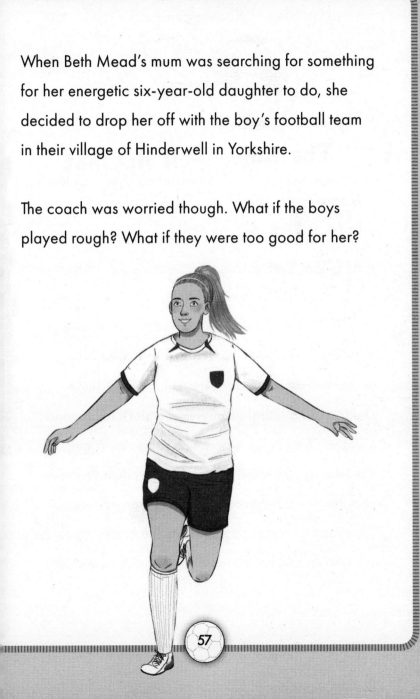

When Beth's mum returned to pick her up, the coach admitted that it had been the other way round. Beth had bossed those boys!

Beth was always up for a challenge. She was the only girl on her primary school football team . . . at first. But her performances encouraged the other girls to join. Beth eventually captained the side.

Her professional career began with Sunderland. With them, she won the Women's Premier League twice, before moving to Arsenal in 2017. There, she formed a lethal partnership with Dutch legend Vivianne Miedema, who became her girlfriend. The pair have already scored 126 Women's Super League goals between them, and many more in European and cup competitions. Beth also holds the all-time record for the most goal assists in the league.

In summer 2021, Beth was shocked to learn that she had not been selected for the GB Olympics squad. She watched as Vivianne went with the Dutch side to Japan and was the tournament's top scorer with ten goals.

> **"You can let these things break you or use them as motivation. It's motivated me to do better on and off the pitch this season."**
>
> – Beth Mead

When the new Women's Super League season began, a month after the Olympics, Beth found herself 'playing angry', determined to prove her doubters wrong. Arsenal finished runners-up to Chelsea by a single point, but Beth topped the assists table and was the third-highest scorer. During the season, she also scored her first hat-trick for England and then bagged a second one a month later.

Her total of 20 goals for England in a single season was a new record by any male or female footballer.

Beth entered EURO 22 in good spirits – but even she couldn't predict just how well it would go . . . She scored yet another hat-trick in the Lionesses' 8–0 thrashing of Norway and her goals, flair and creativity helped drive England to victory. Her six goals and four assists made her the Player of the Tournament, and played a huge part in England winning their first ever EUROs crown.

DID YOU KNOW?

Following Beth's performance at EURO 22, the Coastliner bus company in North Yorkshire named one of its buses 'Beth Mead' in her honour. Sea Life Scarborough did the same with one of its octopuses!

Red Card For Neymar

After a great individual goal for Brazilian side Santos in a 2011 Copa Libertadores game versus Colo-Colo from Mexico, it was time for superstar forward Neymar to celebrate. He put on an upside-down mask of himself, given to him by adoring fans in the stands. The referee didn't see the funny side and showed him a yellow card. It was his second of the game, and so Neymar was given a red card and sent off. Oops!

DID YOU KNOW?

There are many different versions of the game, including deaf football, wheelchair football and football for amputees (people who have lost part or all of a limb) – and the list is growing. The Amputee Football World Cup began in 1984. The 2022 winners were Turkey, who beat Angola 4–1 in the final.

World Cup Chopper

Argentina won the 2022 FIFA World Cup in a gripping 3–3 final that went to a penalty shootout. When they returned home, more than four million people came out onto the streets of Buenos Aires, the capital, to watch Lionel Messi and his teammates in an open-topped bus parade. The streets became so crowded that the bus couldn't move and the players had to be airlifted away by helicopter!

Train-ing Session

Spartak Moscow's team were in trouble before their 2006 UEFA Champions League game against Italian giants Inter Milan. But it wasn't because of an injury crisis . . . No, they were stuck on their team bus in traffic and couldn't get to their own stadium!

Spartak's coach Vladimir Fedotov ordered his players to leave the bus and run almost 2,000m to the closest train station. Coach Vlad then gave his pre-match team talk in a crowded train carriage, packed with other passengers.

The team arrived just in time for kick-off, but all the hoo-ha must have left them flustered, as they let in a goal in the very first minute. The game ended 1–0 to Inter. Gutted!

Incredible Injuries

Football is an action-packed game with high-speed collisions making injuries inevitable. That said, perhaps some of the following footballer injuries could have been avoided . . .

Santiago Cañizares was looking forward to the 2002 World Cup as Spain's first-choice goalkeeper. But he dropped an aftershave bottle on his foot before the tournament. The bottle cut the tendon in his toe, forcing him out of the World Cup and letting a young rival, Iker Casillas, take his place.

England defender Rio Ferdinand was putting his feet up and playing a Pro Evolution Soccer video game. Unfortunately, he strained the tendons in his knee and missed a number of games as a result. Oops!

Manchester United goalkeeper Alex Stepney shouted orders at his defenders so loudly during a 1975 game against Birmingham City, that he dislocated his jaw!

Norwegian defender Svein Grøndalen was out running in the woods in 1980 when he disturbed a sleeping moose which charged at him, causing him to roll down a hill. A nasty cut in Svein's leg kept him out of a World Cup qualifying game against Finland.

In 2021, Tunisian defender Rami Kaib was trying to do the right thing and eat healthily. Whilst chomping down on a raw carrot, he broke his jaw and missed a month's worth of games for his Dutch club, Heerenveen!

Cup (and) Sorcerers

In 1989, Germany was divided into two countries, West and East. West Germany's women's team had made it to the final of the third ever EUROs tournament, where they beat Norway 4–1 to be crowned European champions. Hurrah! But the prize the winning players received from the German FA wasn't a big fat cheque, a car, or even lots of free football kit . . .

No, each player was given a dainty tea service of delicate china plates, cups and saucers, all decorated in pretty flowers. Sexist and shocking!

If anything, the tea service spurred the team on to be taken seriously. Between 1991 and 2013, Germany reached every European Championship, only losing one out of 75 qualifying games – an extraordinary achievement. They won seven of the eight tournaments and, if that wasn't enough, added two World Cup triumphs (2003 and 2007) and an Olympic gold medal as well. When the German team took part in EURO 2022, each player was promised €60,000 if they won the tournament. That's better!

DID YOU KNOW?

Music and reality TV star Chelcee Grimes played football for Liverpool as a junior, and went on to play for Everton, Spurs, Fulham and Tranmere Rovers. Despite a music career which includes writing songs for Dua Lipa, Kesha and Kylie Minogue, Chelcee still plays for Merseyrail Ladies in North West Womens Regional League!

Colour Clash

Germany's Ralf Rangnick is a world-famous coach. He is credited with inventing *gegenpressing*, where a team defends very high up the pitch to win back the ball quickly in order to launch their own attack.

Back in 2006, Ralf was coach of German club TSG 1899 Hoffenheim II. When one of his players kept jogging around at the fringes of the game, and not getting stuck in, Ralf got angry. He shouted at the player to get involved but the player ignored him. Rude!

Or was it? The reason turned out to be simple – the player wasn't a player at all . . . he was the referee! Ralf was colour blind and had confused two colours of kit. Oops!

"We normally play in blue, but were wearing our new red away jerseys and the referee was in dark green. I simply got them mixed up."

Being colour blind certainly didn't hold Ralf back. He went on to manage RB Leipzig, Manchester United and, in 2022, the Austrian national team. And Ralf isn't alone. Lars Lagerbäck is also colour blind and has been manager of Sweden, Nigeria, Iceland and Norway.

DID YOU KNOW?

Jude Bellingham made such a positive impact in his time at Birmingham City that they retired the number 22 shirt he played in after he left for Geman club Borussia Dortmund. Jude was only 17 years old at the time!

Shorts Story

Italy were leading Brazil 1–0 in the 1938 World Cup semi-final when Swiss referee Hans Wüthrich awarded a penalty. Up stepped Italian captain and goal machine Giuseppe Meazza.

But as Giuseppe placed the ball down, the elastic in his shorts broke . . .

. . . and his shorts fell down. Oops!

Cool as you like, Giuseppe held his shorts up with one hand as he took – and scored – the penalty. Italy made it to the final where they won 4–2 over Hungary, with Giuseppe setting up three of his team's goals. Pants-tastic!

Full-Time Teeth

In a 1957 lower league match, Danish team Norager was leading rivals Ebeltoft 4–3 with seconds to go. Referee Henning Erikstrup went to blow the final whistle . . . when his false teeth fell out! Whilst Henning fumbled around to put his teeth back in, the game continued – and during those few seconds, Ebeltoft scored a stunning equaliser, making it 4–4. But the ref was having none of it . . . He disallowed the goal, then, with his teeth back in place, blew the final whistle, giving Norager a 4–3 victory!

Scorpion Attack!

Italy enjoyed competitive women's football long before many other countries. Its top women's league, Serie A, was founded in 1968. One of the undoubted stars in the 1990s and 2000s was Patrizia Panico, nicknamed 'the Scorpion' because she was oh-so deadly in front of goal. How deadly? Well, at AGSM Verona, she scored 34 goals in just 32 league games. At Torino, she bagged 88 goals in 74 games, whilst at Torres she notched up an incredible 175 goals in just 134 games.

In total, Patrizia scored an amazing 647 goals in 656 club games, and that's not all . . . The Scorpion struck 107 times when playing for the Italian national team. What a star!

On retirement in 2016, Patrizia sought out new challenges and turned to coaching. In 2017, the world sat up when she was appointed head coach of Italy's Under-15 boy's team. Under her charge, the team didn't lose a single game, playing 12 matches and winning ten. Three years later, she was made assistant manager of Italy's Under-21 men's team, charged with developing the next generation of Italian superstars.

"I don't mind whether I coach men or women, just that I can pass on my knowledge."

As if to prove it, in 2021 she became head coach of ACF Fiorentina's women's team. Go, Patrizia!

All Change

Boca Juniors is a famous Argentinian football club, home to legendary former players like Diego Maradona and Carlos Tevez. But when they started out in 1905, they couldn't settle on their colours.

They started with a white shirt with thin black stripes then switched to a light blue shirt, then back to another striped shirt, this time with vertical blue stripes. Phew! It seemed like a decision had finally been made.

But there was a new problem . . .

It turned out that another local side, Nottingham de Almagro, had a similar shirt. No! So, the teams decided to play a match with the winner keeping the strip.

Boca lost. But they had a new idea . . . They decided that the next ship that sailed into the local port would provide their new colours. It turned out to be a Swedish ship, named *Drottning Sophia* (meaning 'Queen Sophia').

The blue and yellow of the Swedish flag remain on Boca's shirts and crest to this day. Result!

DID YOU KNOW?

In 2019, Wigan Athletic organised a competition for local schoolchildren to design a mascot. The winners were eight-year-old Cayden and nine-year-old Neve, who led the new mascot out for the club's opening game versus Cardiff City. Their winning design was a pie with arms and legs, called Crusty! Delicious!

Dream Debuts

Name: Marcus Rashford

Born: Manchester, UK, 1997

Country: England

Club: Manchester United

Position: Winger or left-sided attacker

Famous for: Being a pacy, exciting attacker who likes to run at defenders and unleash unstoppable shots

Did you know that Marcus Rashford started out as a goalkeeper, and his hero was Manchester United's American keeper Tim Howard?

Marcus was still at primary school when he was signed by Manchester United's academy. By this time he had already moved out of goal, further up the pitch. He learned some of his attacking tricks and moves by copying players in early versions of FIFA video games.

In 2016, Manchester United had an injury crisis, with 13 first-team players out of action. Eighteen-year-old Marcus was called up to be on the bench for the game and was thrilled. But then, striker Anthony Martial suffered an injury which meant Marcus went from sub to starter, set to make his first team debut in the UEFA Europa League. Wow!

The match was against Danish side Midtjylland and United were 2–1 down from the first leg.

Nothing fazed Marcus, even when United's opponents opened the scoring in the second leg. He managed to score twice in return as United won an easy 5–1 victory. He also beat the legendary George Best's record to become United's youngest ever goal scorer in Europe. Marcus was buzzing!

There was no time to sit back and congratulate himself though. Three days later, Marcus was in action again, this time making his Premier League debut against Arsenal, who were firm favourites to win. Roared on by a passionate home support, he scored in the 29th minute with a shot high into the roof of the goal. Three minutes later, he rose majestically to glance a header into the far corner. Pandemonium! United ran out narrow 3–2 winners and Rashford was the name on everybody's lips – two doubles in two debuts!

"As soon as the ball goes in the back of the net, it's like something goes off in your head. You just want to do it again and again and again. You crave the feeling."

Fast forward just three months and Marcus found himself walking out onto the famous turf of Wembley Stadium. He was now making his debut for England, against Australia . . .

With two and a half minutes of the game gone, Marcus flicked the ball round the corner for Raheem Sterling to run onto. Raheem's attempted cross bounced off an Australian defender and ballooned up into the air. Who was in position as the ball came down? Marcus, of course. He struck the ball on the volley and it flew into the net. He had now scored on THREE memorable debuts. Rashford!

Worth the Wait

Egyptian goalkeeper Essam El-Hadary had always dreamed of playing in a World Cup. Boy, did he have a long wait!

Essam first began playing football on the sly, against his parents' wishes. He would sneak off with his school books as if he was going to study, then playing football instead, washing his muddy clothes in the river before coming home.

Essam was picked to play for the Egyptian national team in 1996, before Bukayo Saka or Marcus Rashford were even born. He enjoyed great continental success with Egypt, playing over 150 times for his country. But despite winning the African Cup of Nations four times, Egypt failed to qualify for

World Cups five times in a row. It looked like Essam would never fulfil his dream . . .

"I felt there was something missing without a World Cup appearance."

Then in 2018 – joy! Egypt finally made it to the World Cup tournament, held in Russia. Essam was now 45 years old. Most players have long since retired by that age, but Essam was still playing and felt sharp. It was headline news when he was selected for the squad, although not as the first-choice keeper. He had to sit on the bench and watch as Egypt lost first to Uruguay, then 3–1 to the hosts.

Egypt were now out of the tournament but still had one more match to play, against Saudi Arabia. It was Essam's moment at last! Selected at the age of 45 years, 161 days, he was the oldest debutant at a World Cup and the oldest ever player!

Essam kept his side in the game with some thrilling saves – none more so than when he dived spectacularly to his right to push away Fahad Al-Muwallad's penalty attempt.

Unfortunately, he couldn't stop a second Saudi penalty, and a heartbreakingly late strike in the fifth minute of added time gave Saudi Arabia a 2–1 victory. But Essam had taken part in a World Cup match and become the first African keeper to save a World Cup penalty. He finally retired from football at the age of 47½. Epic!

DID YOU KNOW?

Essam scored a long-range goal when playing for Al Ahly in the CAF Super Cup final. He struck the ball from deep in his own half. The ball sailed up the pitch, hit the crossbar and bounced off the Kaizer Chiefs' goalkeeper into the net. Boom!

Everyone's Against Us!

Sometimes even the ref and the opposing team's ball boys are against you . . .

A 2006 Brazilian cup game pitted Santacruzense against Atlético Sorocaba. As an attack broke down and the Sorocaba goalkeeper went to take the goal kick, a Santacruzense ball boy cheekily snuck onto the pitch and kicked the ball into the net.

The ref, Silvia Regina de Oliveira, was a top official and the first woman to referee in the Brazilian Serie A championship. Amazingly, she let the goal stand and Santacruzense got away with a cheeky 1–1 draw!

Facing the Music

In 2019, Matthew Stacey stepped in to referee an Essex & Sussex Border League match when the booked referee hadn't arrived. The only trouble was, he didn't have a whistle! The quick-thinking chairman of one of the teams ran to his car and retrieved his son's toy harmonica. Matthew gave a blast on the harmonica every time he needed to start or stop the game!

Taking a Walk

In 2011, John Croot from Chesterfield invented a whole new version of the beautiful game.

Designed to be safe for older people and those with physical disabilities, John's 'walking football' outlawed running, jogging, contact in tackles and sending the ball above head height. Games are usually six-a-side and last 40 minutes in total.

The sport quickly caught on – especially amongst older fans wanting to stay active. It's become so popular that, in 2023, walking football launched its own World Cup tournament with 32 teams taking part!

Sam Scores

Sam Kerr is the only female footballer to be the top scorer in professional leagues in THREE different continents. She achieved the feat twice in the A-League Women (formerly the W-League) in Australia and New Zealand, and three times in the NWSL (National Women's Soccer League) in North America. She moved to the Women's Super League with Chelsea in 2020, and wasted no time making her presence felt. She was the top goal scorer in both the 2020–21 and 2021–22 seasons. Sam has scored nearly 300 goals in her career so far. Lethal!

#1

South Pole Soccer

In 2015, a game of football was held at Union Glacier Camp in Antarctica. This is a stopping-off point for expeditions heading to the South Pole. The players used bamboo poles for the corner flags and formed goals out of skis. The teams were mostly made up of scientists and staff from the camp, but also included legendary England player David Beckham! David's team went 3–0 up early in the game but the match ended in a chilly 3–3 draw.

DID YOU KNOW?

Deep in Finland's most northerly region of Lapland is a fifth division football club called FC Santa Claus. The club's strip is red and white – the traditional colours of Father Christmas – and the club motto is 'Don't stop believing!'.

Strikers in Space

To celebrate the 2014 FIFA World Cup hosted by Brazil, three astronauts on board the International Space Station (ISS) had a football kickabout.

With microgravity in space, the ball and players float around. Astronauts Reid Wiseman, Steve Swanson and Alexander Gerst found that diving saves were easy-peasy!

Four years later, Russian astronauts Anton Shkaplerov and Oleg Artemyev also practised their skills aboard the ISS. They used an official 2018 FIFA World Cup ball (an Adidas Telstar 18). The ball flew more than 50 million km in space whilst orbiting in the ISS – before being taken back down to Earth and used in the first game of the tournament!

Seeking Safety

Name: Nadia Nadim

Born: Herāt, Afghanistan, 1988

Country: Denmark

Clubs: B52 Aalborg, Fortuna Hjørring, IK Skovbakken, Manchester City, Paris Saint-Germain, Portland Thorns FC, Racing Louisville, Sky Blue FC, Team Viborg

Position: Striker

Famous for: An energetic, effective attacker whose story has truly inspired others

Nadia Nadim was born in Herāt, a town in Afghanistan. Her father was a general in the Afghan army but when Nadia was nine, he was captured and killed by the Taliban, a religious group that had taken control of the country. As a girl, Nadia was not allowed to go to school or play in public, and her mother, Hamida, could no longer work as a school principal.

Nadia, her sisters and her mother moved from house to house to escape capture themselves. Survival was their only goal for three long years. Finally, the family did the only thing they could do to safeguard their future – flee Afghanistan.

Their escape involved false passports, a minivan to Pakistan, a flight to Italy and then being trafficked across Europe in cargo trucks. The family were hungry and afraid. They thought they were heading for London but when they were finally allowed out of the truck, they found themselves in a small town in Denmark and were sent to a refugee centre.

It was the first time in years that 12-year-old Nadia had felt safe. And it was the first time she had seen girls playing football. She and her sisters joined in, and were soon playing all day, most days.

"**When I started playing football in a refugee camp, I fell in love with the game. I didn't even know that women footballers could reach this level.**"

- Nadia Nadim

After her family left the centre and settled in Denmark, Nadia kept on playing, for school teams, local clubs and, in 2006, for her first professional club, IK Slovbakken. Her sister, Giti, played for the same team.

Nadia's progress was rapid and, in 2009, she was picked for Denmark. Nadia would play a further 102 times for her adopted country, scoring 38 goals. She has also played for three clubs in the US, in England (Manchester City), and in France (Paris Saint-Germain). Helping PSG topple the formidable Olympique Lyonnais Féminin to win the French league in 2020–21 was one of her proudest football achievements.

Nadia is just as bright off the pitch as on it. She can speak nine languages and studied medicine whilst still playing football. After years of charity and humanitarian work, Nadia won the 2017 Dane of the Year award. Amazing! In 2022, she qualified as a doctor and hopes to become a surgeon when she retires from playing. Another step on Nadia's amazing journey.

Wonder Wiegman

In 2022, at Wembley Stadium, the England Lionesses did what the men's team hasn't managed so far – they won a UEFA European Championship. Well done to the players but also congratulations to their Dutch coach Sarina Wiegman. Sarina became the first person to win back-to-back EUROs with different teams (she coached the Netherlands to glory in 2017) and has never lost a game at the EUROs. In fact, with Sarina in charge, England went two whole years (30 matches) without losing a game. Remarkable!

Super Speedy Salah

Egyptian superstar Mo Salah holds a number of goal scoring records. These include the most goals by an African player in Premier League history (53 and counting) and the most goals in a debut season – a stunning 44 when Mo began playing for Liverpool.

In 2022, marvellous Mo also broke the record for the fastest hat-trick in the UEFA Champions League. He came off the bench to score three goals in just six minutes, 12 seconds, as Liverpool thrashed Glasgow Rangers 7–1. Incredible!

A Bright Future

Linda Caicedo had a brilliant 2019. Firstly, she top-scored in the Liga Femenina, Colombia's highest women's league. Then, she was selected to play for Colombia's national women's team. Linda was only – wait for it – 14! Three years later, she helped Colombia beat Chile, Ecuador and Argentina to reach the final of the 2022 Copa América Femenina. Linda was awarded the Golden Ball as the tournament's best player. Top teenager!

DID YOU KNOW?

Ethan Nwaneri became the youngest player in Premier League history in September 2022. He was 15½ years old when he came on as a substitute during Arsenal's 3–0 away win at Brentford.

Block Party

André Villas-Boas was a football-mad Portuguese boy who lived in the same apartment block in Porto as the city's football club manager, Sir Bobby Robson. After chatting to the 16 year old, Sir Bobby arranged for him to start taking some coaching courses. André was thrilled.

He received his first UEFA Pro Licence, a coaching qualification, whilst still a teenager and became manager of the British Virgin Islands, in the Caribbean, when he was only 21! Just over ten years later, André was back in Portugal, as head coach of Porto. Now a famous international coach, he has managed Chelsea, Spurs, Zenit Saint Petersburg and Marseille. It definitely pays to get to know your neighbours!

Goal's This Way!

After a series of five defeats without scoring
a single goal, fans of German fourth division club
FC Magdeburg decided to help their team out.
A big group of fans each carried a large luminous
cardboard arrow, which they pointed in the direction
of the goal their team was attacking. Would their
players get the hint?! Yes! Attacker Chris Wright
scored with ten minutes to go, breaking the
team's 558-minute goal drought. GOAL!

Unfortunately, their opponents, Berliner AK 07,
scored twice, meaning that Magdeburg
suffered a sixth defeat in a row. Oops!

The Worst Team in the World?

It's not a title you'd want now, is it? Madron FC, from a small Cornish village, were strong contenders during a tough 2010–11 season in Cornwall's Mining League Division 1.

The club had lost a lot of players and were struggling to put out a team at times. Their results were . . . bad. No . . . terrible. Wait . . . make that *catastrophic*.

The season began with a 11–0 defeat to Illogan Rbl Reserves. Things perked up with a 4–1 loss to Sennen FC, but the (mild) improvement was short-lived. The team suffered a 16–0 mauling by St Buryan, followed by a monstrous 29–0 thrashing at the hands of Goonhavern Athletic. And the defeats kept raining in . . .

17–0 v Robartes Arms

27–1 Gwinear Churchtown

27–0 Trevenson United

Then Madron played Illogan Reserves again.
The team couldn't get a full eleven players out
onto the pitch. The result was not pretty . . .

Six Illogan players scored six or more goals each
with their striker, Luke Abbott-Smith, bagging TEN
goals. When the referee blew for full time, the score
was Madron FC nil . . .

. . . Illogan Reserves 55!

OUCH!

**"I know everybody is probably laughing
at us but we will battle on."**
– Alan Davenport, Madron FC club chairman

The battered and bruised team ended the 28-game season with no wins and no draws. They scored 12 goals but let in a whopping 407.

DOUBLE OUCH!

Every new season brings fresh hope for players and fans, and so it was the case with Madron. The first game of the 2011–12 season ended 8–2. But, hey, at least they scored . . . twice! Then, in the next game, against Storm FC, Madron stormed to victory, winning 4–2. Yay! The players performed a lap of honour. Well, you can't blame them, can you? Go, Madron!

> **"The lads went crazy at the final whistle, and why not? It was a big win for them. It's been a long time coming."**
> – Alan Davenport

Íbis Crisis

Never fear, Madron FC, there are other teams who have endured tough runs. Take Íbis Sporting Club, from Paulista in Brazil. They began a losing run in 1980, which lasted three years, 11 months and 26 days! Today, they're an up-and-coming side, winning promotion in 2019. But they still laugh about their poor run from the 1980s. When Lionel Messi left Barcelona in 2019, Íbis jokingly offered to sign him, just as long as he 'didn't score too many goals!'.

DID YOU KNOW?

Few clubs do well in Europe against the mighty Barcelona, but one team has a perfect record, winning every match. That club is Dundee United! The Scottish club has played four, won four, scoring seven goals and letting in two!

Pain For Wain

Referees need to keep their cool even when players moan and whine at them. In a 2005 game between English clubs Peterborough North End and Royal Mail AYL (Association Youth League), referee Andy Wain got tired of all the chirping and criticisms from players. When the North End keeper, Richard McGaffin, made yet another comment, the referee's frustration boiled over. He rushed over and squared up to the goalie. The pair had to be pulled apart by shocked players, worried a fight would break out. "It was totally unprofessional," Andy said later. "If a player did that I would send him off, so I had to go."

That's what happened. Andy showed himself the red card! And with no spare refs around, the game was abandoned. Oops!

World Cup Carli

Name: Carli Lloyd

Born: New Jersey, USA, 1982

Nickname: Captain America

Country: USA

Clubs: Atlanta Beat, Central Jersey Splash, Chicago Red Stars, Houston Dash, Manchester City, New Brunswick Power, New Jersey Wildcats, NJ/NY Gotham FC, Sky Blue FC, South Jersey Banshees, Western New York Flash

Position: Midfielder

Famous for: A serial winner of World Cups and Olympic games medals

Carli Lloyd had a glittering career, winning two Olympic gold medals, scoring 124 goals for the US women's team and twice winning Best FIFA Women's Player Award – given to the best female footballer on the planet.

Carli played a whole bunch of sports as a kid and shone in her school's swimming team. But it was a 1999 Women's World Cup game in New York that changed her life. She watched the US team beat Denmark and enjoyed it so much, she stayed on to see the match that followed, Brazil versus Mexico. From then on, Carli vowed she would become a top footballer.

Six years after making her debut for the US women's national team, Carli helped propel the

US team into the 2011 World Cup final versus Japan. The US were hot favourites but the game ended in a 2–2 draw. A penalty shootout awaited. Abby Wambach scored first for the US but teammate Tobin Heath missed. There was real pressure on the third US penalty taker: Carli.

Carli marched calmly from the halfway line, placed the ball on the spot, stepped back and . . .

. . . blazed the ball high over the bar. Noooo! Japan scored and when another US player missed, the World Cup was Japan's. Heartbreak! "It was a pretty tough thing to go through," recalled Carli. "But I want to go to Canada in 2015 and hold that trophy."

Four years later, Carli was getting close to her dream. She scored in each of the three knockout games that took the US team to the final. Facing them again was Japan. But Carli and her teammates were not in the mood for a repeat defeat. The final was the 202nd time she had played for the US. She used all her experience to prepare.

It paid off. In the third minute, Carli swept the ball with her left foot into the corner of the net. Goal! Her 67th for the US team! She barely had time to celebrate before the game kicked off again. There was a scramble in the Japanese goalmouth and Carli pounced a second time.

"My mind was ready, I was on my toes and anticipated where the ball was going to go and let my instincts do the rest."

Goal! The US were comfortably ahead. But Carli was saving the best for last . . .

In the 16th minute, she ran with the ball towards the halfway line. Seeing Japan's goalkeeper Ayumi Kaihori off her line, she struck the ball 50m up and over the flailing arms of the keeper and into the net.

"Look at that for another magnificent effort. Ohhhh, WHAT A GOAL! Carli Lloyd has a hat-trick!"
– Jonathan Pearce, BBC commentator.

Carli had scored three goals in just 13 minutes. Extraordinary! Japan went on to score, but the US ran out comfortable winners: 5–2. The World Cup was theirs and Carli was made Player of the Match AND the entire tournament. She went on to score in the first two matches of the 2019 World Cup (won once again by the USA), becoming the first player to score in SIX World Cup games in a row. Awesome!

Mascot Madness

The first football team mascots were real-life animals such as Major the Saint Bernard dog (Newton Heath LYR, 1900s – see p14), Hennes the goat (Cologne FC in Germany, 1950s onwards) and Tiddles the cat (Brighton and Hove Albion, 1950s).

In 2010, one real-life mascot, a large eagle, moved clubs from Benfica (Portugal) to Lazio (Italy) for a transfer fee of around £100,000. Yes, really! The eagle is called Olimpia and weighs 12kg. She's a fitting mascot . . . The eagle is a symbol of the club, appearing on the club crest. In fact, Benfica isn't the only club to have a live eagle as a mascot. PFL Ludogorets in Bulgaria is home to an eagle called Fortuna, whilst Club América of Mexico boasts a feathery mascot named Celeste.

The mascots in Major League Soccer (MLS) in North America include Timber Joey of the Portland Timbers. Armed with a real chainsaw, he cuts slices off a tree trunk before each game and presents a piece to the MVP (Most Valuable Player) of each game!

Many mascots are based on cats, dogs, lions or wolves. However, stranger examples include a dinosaur called Gunnersaurus (Arsenal), a bee called Emma (Borussia Dortmund), a gorilla (Perth Glory in Australia), an iguana (Colombia's Deportivo Cali) and even a central heating boiler (West Bromwich Albion)!

Stoke City is a long way from the watering holes of Africa, but since 1997, their matchday mascot has been a Hippo called Pottamus. In 1998, after a string of poor performances, disgruntled fans voted Pottamus their seventh best player of the year!

Golden Oldies

Kazuyoshi Miura is a Japanese striker still playing today. No big deal . . . except that Kazu was playing professional football before Lionel Messi was born!

In the 1980s, there were no major professional football leagues in Japan, so talented teenager Kazu had to go abroad, to Brazil. "My father was in Mexico in 1970 to watch the World Cup. He filmed the matches [in which Brazil starred] by 8mm video camera. From the time I was a little boy, I watched the videos over and over again and wanted to live as a professional player."

Kazu found it hard to settle in Brazil at first. "I couldn't understand the language," he recalled. "And the customs were different, so naturally I felt lonely."

But he threw himself into training, and learning Portuguese so he could make friends. In 1986, he got a move to top Brazilian side Santos, home to Brazilian legend, Pelé – Kazu's idol.

In 1992, Japan launched its J. League (now the J1 League) and Kazu returned home to become one of its stars. He was named Asian Footballer of the Year whilst playing for Verdy Kawasaki (now Tokyo Verdy). Then he played 103 league games for Vissel Kobe (where, for a short time, he played with his elder brother, Yasutoshi) before moving to Yokohama FC in 2005. He also became the first Japanese footballer to play in Italy (at Genoa) and appeared for Dinamo Zagreb in Croatia and Sydney FC in Australia.

Kazu's career peaked with his time as an attacker in the Samurai Blue, Japan's national men's team.

Between 1990 and 2000, he played 89 times and scored an impressive 56 goals. His international career eventually came to an end in 2000, the point at which many footballers start winding down their playing careers. But not King Kazu. He kept on playing season . . . after season . . . after season, spending a total of 17 years at Yokohama FC. In 2020, he became the oldest player to appear in a J. League Cup match. He was 53 years, five months and ten days old.

"For sure, it takes me longer than the younger players to recover. But even though it's very hard, I have this passion of wanting to play, so that keeps me going."

In 2022, Kazu moved to Suzuka Point Getters, a club managed by his brother, Yasutoshi – and he has no thoughts of hanging up his playing boots. Far from it! On 22nd April 2023, he made his debut for Oliveirense, becoming the oldest pro in Portuguese football at 56 years, one month and 24 days. His side won their Portuguese second division match against Académico Viseu 4–1. Wow! Kazu really is unstoppable!

Even more experienced than King Kazu is Robert Carmona. Robert began his professional career in 1976 – and guess what? In 2023, after eight operations and more than 2,200 competitive games, he's still playing! The 60 year old is currently captain of Hacele un Gol a la Vida, in Uruguay's fourth division. He began his career as a midfield playmaker and is now a central defender.

Robert has managed to play games in every season

since 1976 for clubs in Spain, Italy, Uruguay, Argentina and the US. He also holds the record for the longest gap between spells at one football club. He played for Uruguayan team La Luz FC in 1984–85 and returned 24 years later, in 2009. His teammates in his first spell at La Luz had long since retired though. It was their sons who were now lining up alongside Robert!

"In my life there's no such thing as 'can't'. I feel like I've been given a gift and I haven't wasted it. I feel very alive and have the energy of a youngster."

– Robert Carmona

The Best Team in the World?

Who is the most dominant club side in world football? Is it Manchester City? Real Madrid? Barcelona?

It might actually be Olympique Lyonnais Féminin. This women's team has ruled French football for the last two decades, winning 14 league championships in a row, from 2007 to 2020. In 2021, their world was rocked when rivals Paris Saint-Germain scooped the title, but it was business as usual the following year: the team from Lyon went through the whole season without losing a game. What's more, they thrashed PSG 6–1 along the way. Revenge!

Captained by French legend Wendie Renard and boasting talents like German–Hungarian midfielder Dzsenifer Marozsán and Norwegian striker

Ada Hegerberg, OL Féminin has also won the Coupe de France Féminine. On the European stage they also reign surpreme. They are current UEFA Women's Champions League champions, winning the competition eight times in the past 12 years. Few teams get to dominate a continent as well as their own country. Outstanding!

DID YOU KNOW?

The surprise package of the 2022 FIFA World Cup was Morocco. Before Qatar 2022, the 'Atlas Lions', as they are nicknamed, hadn't qualified for a World Cup in the 21st century. They certainly made up for lost time, beating European heavyweights Belgium, Spain and Portugal to reach the semi-final – the first African nation to do so. Go, Lions!

Double Trouble

Twenty-one national teams took part in the 1994 Shell Caribbean Cup. The tournament's rules included an odd one: no game could end in a draw. After full time, a drawn game would go into extra time until another goal was scored. Fair enough, but the really strange thing was that any goal scored in extra time would count as double. The results were . . . interesting!

In their last group game, Barbados knew they needed to beat Grenada by two goals to qualify for the next round. At 2–0, it was all going well for them – until Grenada scored in the 83rd minute. As the game neared the end, Barbados struggled to score again. If the game ended at 2–1, they knew they'd be out of the tournament at full time. So, with just three minutes to go, they scored a deliberate own goal to make it 2–2. It was a cunning plan . . . Now they had 30 minutes of extra time to try to score another goal, which, remember, would count as TWO goals – enough to see them through.

But Grenada were also thinking on their feet. If the game ended 3–2 at full time, *they* would go through, not Barbados. It wouldn't matter if it was a 3–2 win or a 3–2 defeat, they just needed to stop extra time happening. So, can you imagine what they tried to do?

If you guessed 'score an own goal', you'd be right. Or . . . half right!

The last few minutes of the match were bonkers. Barbados players were forced to defend BOTH goals as Grenada tried to score at either end of the pitch! But try as they might, Grenada couldn't find the back of the net. The game went into extra time just as Barbados had planned.

"The game should never be played with so many players running around the field confused."
– James Clarkson, manager of Grenada

During extra time, Barbados centre forward Trevor Thorne belted home the winning goal. Barbados were through! But both sides agreed that the competition's rules were a JOKE. By the time the cup was held the following year, the rules had been changed: one goal, one point! PHEW!

A Mist-See Match

In 1945, the mistiest match ever played took place at White Hart Lane in London (Spurs' old ground). Football had only just restarted in England after World War II, and more than 50,000 fans had gathered, keen to see Arsenal take on Soviet champions Moscow Dynamo.

The match referee, Nikolai Latyshev, spoke Russian and no English, whilst the two English referee's assistants spoke no Russian. But that was the least of their worries. An incredibly thick, dense fog, mixed with soot from the city's many coal-burning fires, descended over the pitch. It became impossible to see the goals from outside the penalty area, or one side of the pitch from the other!

Despite the conditions, the game went ahead. With the fog hiding much of the action from the referee, players broke the rules time and time again. The game was supposed to be a friendly . . . not a chance! Fists, elbows and tackles went flying. Ouch!

At one point, the referee stopped the game just to count how many players were on the pitch. It turned out that the visitors had been sneakily playing 12-a-side with an extra player. Some spectators claimed they had counted up 15 Moscow Dynamo players on the pitch at one point!

"It was the greatest match *never* seen!"

– a spectator at the game

But if you think Arsenal were hard done by, you should know that they weren't playing entirely fair themselves. They had borrowed some top players from other clubs for the match, including England legend Stanley Matthews. And they had an extra player on the pitch too! Their attacker, George Drury, had been sent off by the ref, but, under the cover of the fog, snuck back on!

Dynamo Moscow eventually beat Arsenal 4–3. Worthy winners? At this point, we haven't the foggiest!

They Think It's All Over . . .

Things were tense during a 2017 Thailand Cup semi-final between Bangkok Sport and Satri Angthong. The game was drawn 2–2 and the penalty shootout that followed was going on and on and on . . .

With the scores locked at an incredible 19–19, up stepped a Bangkok Sport player to take *yet another* penalty. Only, this one was different. His shot hit the crossbar and ballooned up in the air. The goalie ran off in wild celebration. Phew!

But as the ball landed, backspin caused it to roll towards the goal. The keeper raced to stop it but – too late! The ball slipped over the line: 20–19 to Bangkok Sport! The next Satri Angthong penalty was missed. Bangkok Sport had won! So, be careful not to celebrate too early – you don't want to take your eye off the ball!

Made in Sialkot

Did you know that two-thirds of the world's footballs are made in just one city – Sialkot in Pakistan?

Football production here is said to have started in 1889, when a British soldier asked a local saddle-maker to repair his punctured leather soccer ball. He was so delighted with the result, he ordered a batch of balls to be made from scratch. Today, more than 200 factories produce over 40 million footballs each year!

Balls made in Sialkot include the Adidas Al Rihla, the official ball of the 2022 FIFA World Cup. Inside its 20 hand-stitched panels is an electronic IMU motion sensor. It detects the ball's precise position 500 times a second and beams data to the computer system used by video assistant referees (VAR). Amazeballs!

Gooooooooooooaaaaalllllllll!

In the distant past, a goal might be celebrated with a raised arm or a handshake with a team-mate. Not any more! Players explode with delight and some perform extraordinary manoeuvres – from somersaults to dance routines, even when they score a consolation goal.

Sometimes, though, these moves backfire . . .

In 2019, Anderson Lopes scored his first goal for his new club Hokkaido Consadole Sapporo in Japan's J1 League. Delighted, he jumped the pitchside barrier – but didn't know there was three metre drop on the other side. THUD! Fortunately, the only part of Anderson that was hurt was his pride. He headed back onto the pitch – and scored a further three goals!

At the 2018 World Cup, Michy Batshuayi celebrated his Belgium team's goal by kicking the ball as hard as he could. It cannoned off the nearby goal post straight into his face.

SMACK!

In 1997, Chelsea's new recruit Celestine Babayaro scored in a pre-season game against Stevenage Town. He attempted a somersault to celebrate . . . and broke his leg. CRUNCH! He didn't play for many months afterwards.

On other occasions, the celebrations are aimed at angering opposing fans, such as when the US's Alex Morgan scored against England at the 2019 Women's World Cup and mimed drinking a cup of tea. Or, when Brazilian player Edmilson Ferreira scored against América Mineiro (nickname: the

Rabbits) pulled out a carrot from his shorts then ate it in front of the furious rival fans!

Celebrations can also get refs annoyed. When Mirko Vučinić scored the winner for Montenegro versus Switzerland in a EURO 2012 qualifying match, he ripped his shorts off and ran around the pitch with them on his head! The referee was not amused and showed Mirko a yellow card.

Some celebrations are just plain funny. Like . . .

Peter Crouch's stiff-armed robot dance after scoring for England against Jamaica in 2006. Crouchy's robot went viral. He reprised a slightly rustier version in 2017, when he became the oldest player to score 100 Premier League goals.

Roger Milla's hips didn't lie as he shimmied and wiggled a joyful dance after scoring for Cameroon at the 1990 World Cup. Roger's goals and moves were enjoyed all over the planet.

But perhaps the most elaborate goal celebrations of all were made in the 2010s by Icelandic club Stjarnan FC. The whole team would join in, miming silly scenes such as catching a large fish . . . racing down bobsleigh tracks . . . ballroom dancing . . . or riding bicycles. Amazing!

Penalty Points

If you ever fail at taking a penalty, don't fret. Even the best players miss. Ask Harry Kane after his crucial 2022 World Cup miss against France, or France's Kingsley Coman and Aurélien Tchouaméni, who both missed in the 2022 World Cup final penalty shootout, handing victory to Argentina. The winning Argentinean team included the great Lionel Messi, who's missed 31 penalties during his career, two more than Cristiano Ronaldo. Even the greatest of the great miss penalties!

Strikers don't always make the best penalty takers. In Brazil, Rogério Ceni was a goalkeeper who played a staggering 1,200 games for São Paulo. Bu that wasn't the most extraordinary thing about him. Rogério was the club's penalty taker for many seasons, scoring 70

times. He'd also trot upfield to take a cheeky free kick
. . . and scored 61 of these as well!

According to Rogério, apart from needing courage,
penalties involve:

**"Physics, because you have to hit the ball
properly, and psychology, because you
have to know where to put it. And you
have to remain calm."**

DID YOU KNOW?

Football had been played for many years
before penalties were invented in 1891.
However, the penalty spot wasn't introduced
until 1902. Before then, players could take
their shot from anywhere along a line
running 11m from the goal.

The Paralympic Pelé

Name: Jeferson da Conceição Goncalves

Born: Candeias, Brazil, 1989

Nickname: Paralympic Pelé

Country: Brazil

Club: IBC (Instituto de Cegos da Bahia)

Position: Winger

Famous for: Raising the profile of blind football, dazzling fans with his skills and becoming a national celebrity in Brazil

Brazilian footballer Jeferson da Conceição Gonçalves was born with a medical condition called glaucoma, which affects a person's eyesight. By the age of seven, Jeferson was completely blind. Already passionate about football, he refused to give up his sport, and learned to play by touch and sound, keeping the ball under close control. One of his favourite drills was dribbling in and out of the chairs and table legs at home, often with his mother chasing him and shouting!

By the age of 17, Jeferson's talent had been spotted and he was selected for Brazil's world-conquering blind football team. This five-a-side sport is played at many competitions, including the Paralympics. It features a sighted goalkeeper and four blind or visually-impaired outfield players, all of whom must wear a blindfold. Players must control, pass and shoot a special football containing noise-making objects.

Jeferson played at both the 2008 Beijing Paralympics and the 2012 London games. At both tournaments he showcased his great skill and awareness, helping Brazil to win. In Brazil he became known as 'Jefinho' and 'the Paralympic Pelé', and his opponents marvelled at his abilities. Former England captain Keryn Seal said, "His basic skills are absolutely incredible – he can dribble at extreme speed and seems to have a sixth sense."

"Football, for me, is everything. Without football, I would not be who I am today. I am a better person thanks to the sport."

– Jeferson da Conceição Gonçalves

At the 2016 games, Brazil cruised through the group stage, which included a 14–1 thrashing of Costa Rica, before struggling against China. They were 1–0 down and in danger of crashing out of the competition until Jeferson struck, not once, but twice. His two brilliantly taken goals propelled Brazil to the final, where they defeated Iran to complete a hat-trick of Paralympic gold medals. There was a fourth victory to celebrate in 2021, as Brazil and Jeferson continued their dominance of the five-a-side game.

> "Playing football is when I feel at my best. I feel totally independent on the pitch and I can do whatever I want."

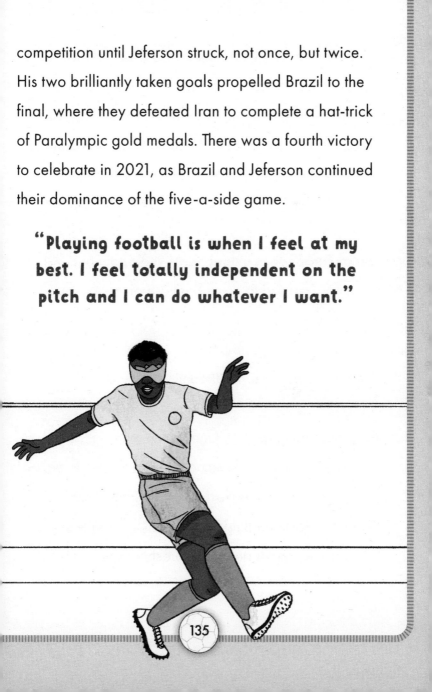

The World Cup Kicks Off!

The first FIFA World Cup was held in 1930, hosted in Uruguay who were Olympic football champions. There had never been a world championship in football before and a host of strange things happened.

Lots of European countries, including Spain and Germany, refused to come because of the expense – and the Romanian team's players were chosen not by a coach or manager but by the country's ruler, King Carol II. It's unusual, we'll admit!

The French, Belgian and Yugoslavian teams all sailed to South America on the same ship, the *Conte Verde*. Along the way, they picked up the Romanian and Brazilian teams. The ship also carried three World Cup referees and the organiser, Jules Rimet, who had the

World Cup trophy in his suitcase. The voyage took 15 days and players kept fit by running round the deck. In the evenings, they were entertained by a string quartet!

Argentina's star forward, Manuel Ferreira, had to leave the tournament to go back to university to take an exam. Boo! A new player called Guillermo Stábile was called up to take his place. Goal-grabbing Guillermo ended up being the leading scorer with an impressive eight goals.

The strange stuff continued all the way to the final, featuring Argentina and Uruguay. The two teams both threw tantrums . . . over the ball! Each side wanted to play with a different type of ball, so the referee, John Langenus, came up with a diplomatic solution: two balls. One would be supplied by Argentina for the first half, and one from Uruguay for the second.

Speaking of Mr Langenus . . . This history-making ref wasn't dressed like referees today. He refereed the first ever World Cup final wearing a crisp white shirt, a tie, a jacket and wide, flappy plus-four trousers tucked into his long socks!

Uruguay triumphed 4–2 in the final, their last goal scored by star striker Héctor Castro. The players sadly didn't get the chance to defend the trophy though. Annoyed at the lack of European teams entering their tournament, Uruguay refused to send a team to the next World Cup in Italy. Oh dear – snubbed!

DID YOU KNOW?

Héctor Castro lost his right arm in an accident with an electric saw when he was 13 years old. That didn't stop him scoring 18 goals in 25 international games. Bravo, Héctor!

Fantastical Fees

Top players today move from one club to another often for eye-watering transfer fees. Think of Jack Grealish, who moved from Aston Villa to Manchester City in 2021 for a cool £100 million. Or French striker Kylian Mbappé who cost Paris Saint-Germain around £160 million to buy from Barcelona in 2017.

Not all players go for big money though. Some are real bargains, such as Riyad Mahrez, bought by Leicester City from French club Le Havre for just £450,000. After four seasons and a Premier League championship with Leicester, Mahrez was sold to Manchester City for – wait for it – a whopping £60 million!

But none can compete with Portuguese club Sporting Lisbon, who paid around £1,500 in 1997 for a young

Cristiano Ronaldo. Bargain of the century!

Not all transfers even involve money. Here are four of the funniest fees paid for footballers . . .

Hugh McLenahan was a hotshot half back (an early type of midfielder) who played at Stockport County. In 1927, Manchester United wanted to buy him, and their assistant manager, Louis Rocca, provided the cash. Louis also ran an ice cream business – so he added a couple of freezers full of ice cream to the fee. No one knows if wafers and cornets were thrown in!

Chilean attacker Franco Di Santo was bought by Audax Italiano in exchange for two football goal nets and 40 litres of paint. Useful! In 2008, the club sold him to Chelsea for £3.4 million – quite a profit!

Di Santo went on to win the FA Cup with Wigan, and play for Werder Bremen and FC Schalke 04 in the top German league, the Bundesliga.

In 2006, Marius Cioară was a defender for Romanian club UT Arad, until they sold him to another Romanian club, Regal Horia, for 15kg of pork sausages! Marius was enraged at the insulting fee. He quit football and went to work on a farm in Spain. His new club were furious and tried to get their bangers back!

Finally, let's look at one of the fishiest transfers in 21st-century football. It involved two Norwegian third division teams, Floey and Vindbjart. In 2002, Floey signed striker Kenneth Kristensen from Vindbjart. Floey *shelled out* the agreed fee – the player's weight (about 75kg) in fresh shrimp! Great catch!

The British Independents

After the England men's team won the World Cup in 1966, interest in football rocketed in Britain, amongst girls as well as boys. The only problem was that girls and women weren't allowed to play at men's football club grounds. The FA had imposed this ban in 1921, following World War I. Unfair!

Leah Caleb and Chris Lockwood were typical of a lot of football-mad girls at the time, playing playground games with boys but wishing they had a team of their own. Leah's idol was George Best and she tried to play like him, turning and jinking past defenders to set up or score goals.

Leah was just 12 and Chris 14 years old when they got the chance to play for Chiltern Valley Ladies, a team based in Luton. Like many other ladies teams, they had to find parks to play in, and get changed in toilets or scout huts before matches. The team was run by bus driver Harry Batt and his wife, June. "Harry really was a visionary and a maverick," said Leah, years later. "His belief in the women's game at that time was incredible."

In 1971, Harry's team got a golden opportunity when an unofficial Women's World Cup was organised in Mexico and they were invited to compete. Harry selected a 14-player squad, mostly drawn from Chiltern Valley Ladies. The English FA didn't help at all and Harry couldn't even call the team 'England'. He settled for the name 'British Independents'.

Amongst the players selected were Leah and Chris. Neither girl had been on a plane before – and when their plane touched down in Mexico, they couldn't believe the reception. Hundreds of cheering Mexican fans had turned out to greet them – it was as if there was a celebrity flying with them. Then Chris realised: "It was us! We couldn't believe it. It was like going into the TARDIS and coming out in another world."

Leah and Chris were equally surprised to find crowds of fans coming to watch their training sessions and waiting outside their hotel, handing them bouquets of flowers and other gifts. The two girls were even invited to appear on Mexican TV. They were famous!

They also were impressed by how fit and well-drilled the other teams at the tournament were. It seemed that women's football was taken seriously in other countries. Compared to the lack of interest at home, the players were astonished by the warm welcome they received.

That welcome didn't extend out onto the pitch however. During their first match, the girls were overwhelmed both by the massive Azteca Stadium in Mexico City, and by their strong, physical opponents, Argentina. Captain Carol Wilson broke a bone in her foot. She played on but her team were no match for Argentina, who won 4–1.

> **"You can't imagine the noise! You couldn't help but get nervous because you'd never experienced anything like it. You felt tiny."**
> – Janice Emms, British Independents player

Bruised and tired, the team had less than 18 hours to recover before their next game, against the hosts, Mexico. This time the Azteca was nearly full, with over 90,000 fans crammed into its giant concrete bowl. With lots of injured players – and struggling in the intense heat – the British Independents were defeated easily by their skilled and well-coached opponents. Leah and Chris's World Cup dreams were over.

Back at the hotel, the Mexican team laid on a party for the English players. A Mexican fan presented them with a homemade banner, written in his best English:

England
You have lost
the play
but you have
get the
heart of Mexico.

Although they had lost their matches, the support the team had received at the tournament made the trip truly memorable. "We wouldn't have changed our experience for anything, the Mexican people really embraced us," said Leah.

The British Independents returned home – but this time there were no cheering fans. Instead there were punishments. Leah and Chris received a three-month ban from playing whilst older members of the team received six-month bans. Poor Harry, the team manager, was banned for life from running or coaching a football team. He was heartbroken.

Later in 1971, the FA removed their ban on women's football, and an England team played their first official international game against Scotland in 1972. As the years went by, the story of the British Independents was lost.

By 2019, women's football was booming, with 160 countries attempting to qualify for the eighth FIFA

Women's World Cup. In the same year, Chris, Leah and the rest of the team held a reunion. This time, their story captured the interest of the media, featuring in newspapers and on TV. They even got a video message from legendary former Lioness and EURO 2022 winner Jill Scott:

> **"You really have paved the way for us. Without you, we wouldn't be here today having the career that we absolutely love."**

Getting Shirty

A player taking their shirt off for a goal celebration equals a yellow card – but French forward Eric Hassli thought he'd found a way round the law . . .

In a 2011 Major League Soccer (MLS) game for the Vancouver Whitecaps, Eric, who was already on one yellow card, scored and celebrated. He ripped his shirt off . . . only to reveal a second identical one underneath.

However, it didn't stop Referee Baldomero Toledo applying the law: Eric 'two shirts' Hassli had still taken his top off. He was shown a second yellow and sent off!

Striker Parr Excellence

Name: Lily Parr

Born: St Helens, UK, 1905

Country: England

Clubs: Dick, Kerr Ladies FC, St Helens Ladies FC

Position: Attacker

Famous for: Her thunderous shot, prolific goalscoring, and spearheading the super-successful Dick, Kerr Ladies team

During World War I, many British women entered factories to take the places of men sent to join the Armed Forces. The English town of Preston was home to the Dick, Kerr & Co. factory, and in 1917 a group of female workers decided to form a women's football team: Dick Kerr Ladies.

Fourteen-year-old Lily Parr often played football and rugby with her brothers in nearby St Helens. After being spotted in action, Lily was asked to join Dick, Kerr Ladies. She was also offered a job in the factory plus 10 shillings (worth over £25 in today's money) for every game she played.

Parr proved a natural. She was tall, strong and had a shot as hard, if not harder, than many male players. In her first season, she scored 43 goals. By the time she retired in 1951, she had scored almost a thousand!

Dick, Kerr Ladies played lots of exhibition games for charity. In 1921, they played in front of 900,000 spectators, raising thousands of pounds. But the growing popularity of the women's game worried the stuffy, sexist men who ran English football. That same year, they banned women from playing matches on professional pitches. The ban stayed in place for 50 years. Shocking!

> **"The game of football is quite unsuitable for females and ought not to be encouraged."**
> – English FA, 1921

Lily and her teammates didn't give up. In 1922, they went on tour to America and Canada, where they played, and often defeated, men's teams. The team was renamed Preston Ladies in 1926 and Parr remained with them, despite leaving her factory job to become a nurse. Sadly the team folded in 1965, just a few years before the FA ban was lifted. But everyone connected with this extraordinary side could be incredibly proud of their record:

Played: 833 games

Won: 759

Drew: 46

Lost: 28

At Last, Leo!

Name: Lionel Messi

Born: Rosario, Argentina, 1987

Nickname: La Pulga ('the Flea')

Country: Argentina

Clubs: Barcelona, Paris Saint-Germain

Position: Forward

Famous for: Being one of the greatest footballers of all time, with dazzling displays of skill, control and creativity, record-breaking goalscoring and frequently assisting other player's goals.

When Lionel 'Leo' Messi finally lifted the World Cup trophy in Qatar in 2022, many fans felt that the little Argentinean had 'completed' football. Game Over. No more levels to reach.

Before he joined French club Paris Saint-Germain in 2021, Leo had spent the majority of his career lighting up the Barcelona team with his vision, flair, incredible goal scoring feats and out-of-this-world dribbling prowess. No one could wriggle and shimmy their way through a crowded defence like Leo.

"I'm happy with a ball at my feet. My motivation comes from playing the game I love."

In fact, the ball seemed *glued* to Leo's feet as he jinked and turned past defenders, twisting them this way and that, and using deceptive bursts of pace.

As his former teammate-turned-mega-manager, Pep Guardiola, put it: "Messi is the only player that runs faster with the ball than he does without it."

In a long career at Barcelona, Leo managed to garner an astonishing array of awards, records and trophies, including:

- Ten La Liga (Spanish league) titles and seven Copa del Rey (Spanish Cup) wins.
- The most goals ever scored in La Liga (474) and the most hat-tricks (36).
- Four UEFA Champions League titles – and the first player to score five goals in a single Champions League game.
- Three UEFA Super Cups and three FIFA Club World Cups.
- SEVEN World Player of the Year awards.

With Argentina, though, it was a different story. Sure, Leo had scored more than 90 goals for his country and won an Olympic gold medal as part of an Under-23s team in 2008, but internationally, the trophy cabinet was bare.

Well, not quite . . . It was packed full of runners-up medals! Four times, Leo and Argentina had reached the final of a major competition, such as a Copa América or World Cup, and on each occasion, he and his teammates had had to settle for second best.

After the fourth time – a loss in the 2017 Copa América final to Chile – Leo announced his retirement from international football. Argentina was shocked and social media was flooded with pleas from fans for him to reconsider. The mayor of Buenos Aires unveiled a new statue of Leo, whilst the president of the country begged him not to quit.

Thankfully, he changed his mind. At the 2021 Copa América, Leo was at his bewitching best. He was joint top goal scorer and voted the tournament's Most Valuable Player. He also passed 150 caps for Argentina, the first footballer to do so. Of Argentina's 11 goals in the competition, Leo scored or assisted nine of them.

He did not score in the final, but his teammate, Ángel Di María, did – delivering a 1–0 victory over Brazil. As the final whistle blew, Leo sank to his knees. Argentina and Lionel Messi had finally won. They were champions of South America for the first time since 1993. A year later, they would be champions of the world, and Leo could enjoy his long-overdue victory!

> **"I have peace of mind of having achieved the dream that has been denied to me so many times."**

DID YOU KNOW?

Lionel Messi's first contract was written on a paper napkin! Barcelona scout Carles Rexach was so excited when first he saw 12-year-old Leo play that he grabbed a pen and the closest thing to a piece of paper – and wrote his contract there and then!

How to Play: Basics

Could YOU be the next Marcus Rashford, Kylian Mbappé or Beth Mead? Maybe you're playing football already, at school, with friends or on a local team. But if you're new to the game, here are a few basics to get you started . . .

Football is played between two teams of 11 players. It's usually played on a grass pitch, divided into sections with a goal at each end. Teams try to score into the opposing team's goal, and the winning team is the one that scores the most goals. A game can end in a 'draw' if both teams end up with the same score. If neither team scores a goal, the score is 'nil-nil' (0–0).

The beginning of the match is called the **kick-off**, and takes place in the middle of the pitch. Competitive games begin with a coin toss to decide which team will start with the ball.

Once the game has begun, players move the ball around the pitch, kicking, dribbling or passing it to other members of their team. They can't use their hands and arms, apart from the goalkeeper, who can use their hands within their penalty area.

Players have different roles, or positions, within the team. These include **attackers** (whose job is to get the ball past the opposite team's defenders and score goals), **defenders** (who try to stop the opposite team from scoring), **midfielders** (who usually play in both attack and defence) and the **goalkeeper** (who defends the goal).

Standard football matches last for 90 minutes, divided into two halves. At the end of the first half, a break called '**half time**' is taken. If the play has been stopped, for example because a player is injured, extra playing time is added at the end of the each half ('**added time**'). The end of the match is called **full time**.

A match can also go into added time in a knockout stage game that has to have a winner, and the score is equal at the end of the game. If there is still no winner, the match goes to a penalty shootout: the two teams take turns aiming at the goal with just the opposing goalkeeper to defend it.

Football games are supervised by a **referee**, who is on the pitch at all times during the match, watching to make sure the rules are being followed. The ref makes decisions and issues warnings such as yellow cards or red cards if a **foul** takes place. The referee is supported by **assistant referees**, and sometimes by a **virtual assistant referee** (VAR).

The referee blows a whistle to stop play or end the game.

DID YOU KNOW?

In a competitive match, the team that loses the coin toss must stand outside of the centre circle when the referee blows their whistle to start the match.

Glossary

ADDED TIME If time has been lost during the game because of injuries, substitutions or other stoppages, it is added at the end of each half. If a match requires a winner, up to 30 minutes of extra time can be added to a drawn game, to give the teams a chance to score.

ASSIST When a player helps another player score a goal, for example by passing to a striker in a good scoring position.

ASSISTANT REFEREE An official who assists the referee, including indicating when the ball goes over the touchline and is out of play, or a player is offside.

BENCH A manager selects additional players, who may be sent on as substitutes during the match. They sit on the 'bench' until they are needed.

CAPTAIN The player selected by the manager to lead the team.

CORNER KICK A way of restarting play. A corner kick is awarded when the ball passes over the goal line without a goal being scored, and the last touch of the ball was by a defending player.

CROSSBAR The pole that runs across the top of a goal, between the vertical goalposts.

DEFENDER A player whose main job is to prevent players from the opposing team from scoring goals.

DRIBBLING When a player runs with the ball, keeping it close to their body to prevent it being intercepted by opposing players.

DROP KICK When a goalkeeper drops the ball, then kicks it down the pitch, as far as possible from the goal.

FEINT When a player acts as if they are going to move or pass in a certain direction, then suddenly changes direction to confuse the opposition.

FIFA The Fédération Internationale de Football Association, the official governing body of international football, established in 1904.

FOUL When a player acts or plays in a way that the referee decides is against the rules.

FREE KICK When a player fouls, a free kick may be awarded to the opposing team.

FULL TIME The end of the game, when the referee blows the final whistle. Full time happens after 90 minutes plus added time.

GOAL The net at each end of a football pitch, held in place by two goalposts and a crossbar. Players try to kick the ball into the other team's goal to score.

GOAL LINE The line that the ball must cross in order for a goal to be scored.

GOALKEEPER Also called a 'goalie' or 'keeper', this player stands in or in front of their goal and tries to stop the ball from entering.

HALF TIME A break that takes place after the first 45 minutes of a football match.

HANDBALL A type of foul where a player touches the ball with their hand or hands.

HAT-TRICK When a player scores three goals in one match.

HEADER When a player uses their head to hit the ball.

KICK-OFF The action of starting play at the beginning of the match or half, or after a goal has been scored.

MANAGER The person in charge of the team, responsible for picking and training players and deciding the playing strategy.

MARKING Following an opposing player closely to try and stop them receiving or passing the ball.

MIDFIELDER A player positioned near the middle of the pitch. They often play in both attack and defence.

OFFSIDE When a player is in the opposing team's half of the field and is nearer to the opposing goal line than both the ball and the second-to-last opposing player.

OWN GOAL When a player on the defending team accidentally scores into their own goal, causing a goal to be awarded to their opponents.

PASS When a player kicks the ball to another player.

PENALTY KICK When a team is awarded a shot at goal, taken from the penalty spot, with only the goalkeeper to defend it.

PENALTY SHOOTOUT These take place in knockout games, where a draw is not allowed. If the score is even after 120 minutes of play, a penalty shootout takes place. Both teams choose five players to take a shot at goal with only the goalkeeper to defend. If the scores are still tied after five penalty kicks each, the shootout goes into 'sudden death': there is a winner once one team scores and the other fails to equalise.

POSSESSION Keeping control of the ball, without it being intercepted by the opposing team.

RED CARD A card that the referee shows to a player to send them off the pitch.

REFEREE A football umpire who starts and ends the game and enforces the rules.

SAVE When the goalie stops the ball from entering the goal, preventing the opposition from scoring.

SHOOTING Attempting to kick the ball into the goal.

STRIKER A player whose key role is to take shots on goal.

SUBSTITUTION When a player is taken off the pitch and swapped for a different player on the team.

TACKLE When a player tries to get the ball from another player.

VAR Video assistant referee. Video technology that helps the referee on the pitch to make fair decisions.

WINGER A player who mostly plays along one side of the pitch.

YELLOW CARD A card that the referee shows to a player to caution them after a foul. Two yellow cards automatically result in a red card, which means the player will be sent off.

Test Your Knowledge

FIND THE ANSWERS ON PAGE 173.

1. Who coached England's Lionesses for two years without losing a single game?

2. In which year was the first FIFA World Cup held, and which country hosted it?

3. Who was the first Black footballer to play for England?

4. Which former England player joined scientists and staff to play football in Antartica in 2015?

5. Which Scottish club has never lost against Barcelona?

6. Which speedy striker reached a top speed that was faster than Usain Bolt's average speed when he broke the 100m sprint record?

7. What is the nickname of the Turkish team that play in a stadium shaped like a crocodile?

8. Who is the only female player to have won World Player of the Year five times in a row?

9. Which Danish player started life as a child refugee, fleeing from Afghanistan with her family?

10. Who was the youngest player ever to win the World Cup, and at what age?

11. What is the name of the mascot designed by local schoolchildren for Wigan Athletic?

12. Which England women's superstar had an octopus named after her?

13. Which African team surprised fans by reaching the 2022 World Cup semi-final for the first time?

14. Which country produces two-thirds of the world's footballs?

15. How old was Ethan Nwaneri when he first played for Arsenal in the Premier League?

16. What was the name of the team who travelled to Mexico to play in the unofficial Women's World Cup in 1971?

17. Whose first contract as a footballer was written on a paper napkin?

18. What is the name of the dog who helped save Manchester United?

19. Which Norwegian player scored nine goals in an Under-20s World Cup match in 2019?

20. Which London club rejected a young Harry Kane, who later moved to Tottenham Hotspur?

Test Your Knowledge answers:

1. Sarina Wiegman (page 94)
2. 1930, hosted by Uruguay (page 136)
3. Benjamin Odeje (page 36)
4. David Beckham (page 88)
5. Dundee United (page 102)
6. Kylian Mbappé (page 13)
7. The Green Crocodiles (page 39)
8. Marta Vieira da Silva (page 42)
9. Nadia Nadim (page 90)
10. Pelé, aged 17 (page 46)
11. Crusty (page 61)
12. Beth Mead (page 60)
13. Morocco (page 117)
14. Pakistan (page 125)
15. 15½ (page 96)
16. The British Independents (page 142)
17. Lionel Messi (page 154)
18. Major (page 14)
19. Erling Braut Haaland (page 40)
20. Arsenal (page 95)

Look out for more fun-filled books from Farshore!

Incredible Sports

Amazing Facts

Amazing Football Facts

CLIVE GIFFORD is an award-winning author of more than 200 books, including *World of Football*, *The Football Encyclopedia* and *Football Record Breakers*. His books have won the Blue Peter Children's Book Award, the Royal Society Young People's Book Prize, the School Library Association's Information Book Award and Smithsonian Museum's Notable Books For Children. Clive now lives in Manchester, a short walk from Manchester United's Old Trafford ground, but remains a lifelong QPR fan. C'mon U Rrrrrs!

LU ANDRADE is an illustrator from Ecuador, currently living in the mountains of Quito. She has studied everything from cinematography to graphic design. After focusing on digital animation for four years, she turned her hand to illustration, working on projects including *Good Night Stories for Rebel Girls*.